Series Editor: JE

98/09

Books are to be returned on or before
the last date below.

LIBREX —

CW00859726

301   £4.99

POPL
SET

: Taylor

RINGWOOD SCHOOL
GRANT MAINTAINED COMPREHENSIVE
LIBRARY

Hodder & Stoughton
A MEMBER OF THE HODDER HEADLINE GROUP

Orders: please contact Bookpoint Ltd, 39 Milton Park, Abingdon, Oxon OX14 4TD. Telephone: (44) 01235 400414, Fax: (44) 01235 400454. Lines are open from 9.00 – 6.00, Monday to Saturday, with a 24 hour message answering service. Email address: orders@bookpoint.co.uk

British Library Cataloguing in Publication Data
A catalogue record for this title is available from The British Library

ISBN 0 340 70195 1

First published 1998
Impression number   10 9 8 7 6 5 4 3 2 1
Year   2002   2001   2000   1999   1998

Copyright © 1998 Liz Taylor

All rights reserved. No part of this publication may be reproduced or transmitted in any form or by any means, electronic or mechanical, including photocopy, recording, or any information storage and retrieval system, without permission in writing from the publisher or under licence from the Copyright Licensing Agency Limited. Further details of such licences (for reprographic reproduction) may be obtained from the Copyright Licensing Agency Limited, of 90 Tottenham Court Road, London W1P 9HE.

Typeset by Wearset, Boldon, Tyne and Wear.
Printed in Hong Kong for Hodder & Stoughton Educational, a division of Hodder Headline Plc, 338 Euston Road, London NW1 3BH by Colorcraft Ltd.

CONTENTS

Glossary

Apartheid – a system where people were treated differently according to their colour

Bipolar analysis – a way of giving a thing or place a score to work out how much you like it

Birth rate – the number of babies born each year for each 1000 people in an area

Bypass – a road enabling through traffic to avoid the city centre

Central Business District (CBD) – where shops and offices are located

City – an urban area which is bigger than a town but smaller than a conurbation

Civil war – a war between different groups of people within one country

Clustered – in groups or clumps

Commercial areas – areas of shops and offices

Communism – a political system based on common ownership of resources

Commuter villages – villages where the majority of the population commute to work

Commuting – travelling to work in another place

Conurbation – a large urban area made up of a number of smaller urban areas

Counterurbanisation – the growth of rural settlements

Crofts – farms where most of the produce is consumed by the owner

Death rate – the number of people dying each year for every 1000 people in an area

Delta – a triangular area of low-lying land at the mouth of a river

Depopulation – a drop in the number of people living in an area

Distribution – how something is spread across an area

Emigration – when a person moves out of a country

Ethnic group – a group of people who all come from the same area

Function – the purpose of a settlement

Gentrification – when improved housing raises the quality of an area

Green Belt – an area around the edge of an urban area where it is difficult to obtain planning permission

Hamlet – a rural settlement which is bigger than a village

Hierarchy – the ordering of places based on what they offer

High-density – packed together e.g. housing

High-order services – specialised services such as an optician

High-tech industry – modern, scientific research and manufacturing

Human – things to do with people such as jobs

Image – a perception of what a thing or place is like

Immigration – when a person moves into a country

Industrial areas – areas of factories or workshops

Industrial Revolution – period of rapid development of industry – from the mid-Eighteenth to mid-Nineteenth centuries

Infant mortality rate – the proportion of babies in a place who die before their first birthday

Informal services – services which are not declared to the authorities and taxed, such as selling goods on the street

In-migration – moving into an area

Irrigation – when farmland is artificially supplied with water

Land use – categories to show how land is used

Less Economically Developed Countries (LEDCs) – poorer countries such as Ethiopia

Life expectancy – the average length of time that people live

Linear – in lines

Literacy rate – the proportion of a population who can read and write

Location – where a place is

Low order services – more general services such as a village shop selling a range of goods

Market – the people who want to buy a particular thing **or** a collection of stalls used for selling

Mental map – an individual knowledge of a place

Migration – when a person moves home with the intention of staying in their new location

More Economically Developed Countries (MEDCs) – richer countries such as the USA

Natural increase – growth in a population through births

Out-migration – people moving away from an area

Pedestrianisation – when vehicles are banned from roads to allow people to walk freely

Physical – natural features and events

Physical area – the amount of space a thing or place takes up

Physical Quality of Life Index (PQLI) – a way of giving countries a score according to information about the quality of life of their population

Population – the people who live in a place

Primary industry – jobs involving obtaining natural materials (e.g. mining)

Public Enquiry – A process where a planning issue is debated

Pull factors – reasons why someone wants to move to a new place

Push factors – reasons why someone wants to move away from their current home

Quality of life – living conditions and lifestyle

Random – with no obvious pattern

Refugee – someone forced away from their home

Relief – the shape of the land

Resident – someone who lives in a place

Residential areas – areas of housing

Retail – shops

Ring Road – see bypass

Rural – a country area

Rural-to-urban migration – movement from the countryside to an urban area

Rural-urban fringe – area on the edges of towns and cities

Secondary industry – making things, e.g. work in a car factory

Services – facilities that people provide for other people

Settlement – A place where people live such as a village, town

Shanty towns – areas of poor quality housing

Specialised services – jobs which concentrate on one aspect of a service such as an optician (one aspect of healthcare)

Squatter settlements – see shanty towns

Suburbanisation – the outward growth of urban areas

Suburbs – an area of relatively low density housing

Tertiary industry – service jobs

Town – a small urban area

Urban – a built up area such as a town or city

Village – a rural settlement which is bigger than a hamlet

SETTLING DOWN

Key Idea

People live in an incredible variety of places. Some people live in crowded cities, whilst others could walk for days without seeing another person. Some people have lived in the same place all their life, whilst others are always on the move. In this book we will learn about the world's population and settlement – people and where they live.

Hello! I'm Peter. My parents are farmers and my family has lived in this house for a long time. It's pretty and quiet here, but my friends live quite a long way away and there's not much to do in the evenings.

Hello! My name's Amit. My area has many old and beautiful buildings. The schools and colleges are good here, and I have lots of friends nearby. There's quite a bit of pollution from the traffic though.

RESOURCE 1.3
Singapore.

Hi! I'm Sally. It's very busy and noisy where I live, but there's always lots to do and see. My family's flat is quite small because land is really expensive here.

RESOURCE 1.1
Oxford, UK.

RESOURCE 1.2
Refugee camp in Palestine.

RESOURCE 1.4
Germany.

Hello! My name's Eva. We came here because we were forced to move away from our old house. We don't have many things with us, but at least my family is together. I hope we will move back some day.

Work through these activities with a partner or in a small group:

1. Match up each of the people above with the place where they live.

2. Divide the photos (Resources 1.1–1.4) into two groups and explain why you put each photo in those groups.

What are rural and urban settlements?

A **settlement** is a place where people live. **Rural** settlements are country villages and **hamlets**, whilst **urban** settlements are **towns** and **cities**. When you looked at the photographs on page 1, you may have divided them into rural and urban. It can be hard to decide what makes a settlement a rural village as opposed to an urban town.

RESOURCE 1.5
Housing estate, Leybourne.

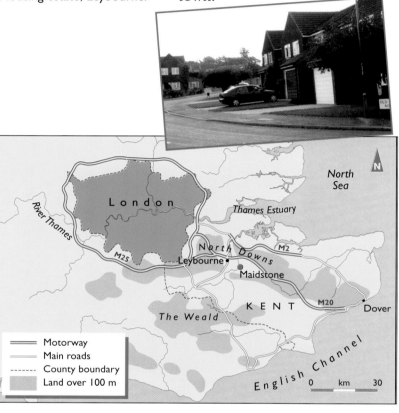

Resource 1.5 shows part of a large housing estate at Leybourne, near Maidstone in Kent. From the evidence in the photo, would you say it is rural or urban? Would you need any further information? We can look at various aspects of a settlement to help us decide whether it is rural or urban. These aspects include:

- the size of the settlement
- the range and type of **services** available
- the types of jobs the **residents** do.

Over the next few pages, we will gather information on each of these three aspects for Leybourne to help you decide whether it is a rural or urban settlement.

RESOURCE 1.6
Location of Leybourne.

3. Describe the location of Leybourne. Use Resource 1.6 and try to give at least five different pieces of information.

LOCATION means where a place is. To describe the location of somewhere, you can:

- use compass directions to say what part of the area it's in e.g. Cardiff is in the south of Wales
- name features the place is located on or near e.g. London is on the River Thames.
- give accurate distances e.g. Barnsley is 20 km north of Sheffield

Settlement Size

If someone asked you how big London is, what would you say? Two ways of measuring the size of a settlement are its **population** – the number of people that live there and its **physical area** – the amount of space it takes up. Settlements come in lots of different sizes, from a single farmhouse in the Scottish highlands up to Mexico City where 18.7 million people live. The largest settlements in Britain are called **conurbations**. This is the name for cities which have grown and joined up with other nearby settlements to create a massive urban area such as London and Glasgow. Urban settlements are larger than rural settlements. However, it's difficult to say exactly how big a settlement needs to be to be called urban, especially if it has joined on to other settlements. Work through the activities to see how Leybourne measures up!

RESOURCE 1.7
Leybourne's population.

Year	Population
1891	270
1921	335
1951	1653
1961	2103
1981	1670
1988	3400 (est.)
1996	3200 (est.)

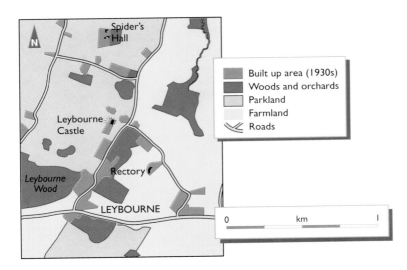

Built up area (1930s)
Woods and orchards
Parkland
Farmland
Roads

Spider's Hall
Leybourne Castle
Leybourne Wood
Rectory
LEYBOURNE

0   km   1

RESOURCE 1.9
Map showing
Leybourne in 1936.

RESOURCE 1.8
Settlement size.

Hamlet	11–100
Small village	101–500
Large village	501–2000
Small town	2001–10 000
Large town	10 001–100 000
City	100 001–1 million

4. Use the figures in Resource 1.7 to draw a line graph showing the growth of Leybourne's population over time.

5. According to the definitions in Resource 1.8, what type of settlement was Leybourne in 1996? Has it always been this type of settlement?

6. Can you think of any problems with using population size as the only way of deciding whether a settlement is urban or rural?

RESOURCE 1.10a
OS map.

<u>Scale</u>
4 cm = 1 km

N

PUBLIC RIGHTS OF WAY

(Not applicable to Scotland)
Public rights of way shown on this map may not be evident on the ground

- - - - - - - - } Public paths { Footpath
                                   Bridleway

Information not available
in uncoloured areas

DANGER AREA
Firing and test ranges in the area
Danger!
Observe warning notices

+ + + + +   Byway open to all traffic
· + · + · +   Road used as a public path

Public rights of way indicated by these symbols have been derived from Definitive Maps as amended by later enactments or instruments
held by Ordnance Survey on 1st Jul 1992 and are shown subject to the limitations imposed by the scale of mapping. Later information
may be obtained from the appropriate County or London Borough Council

The representation on this map of any other road, track or path is no evidence of the existence of a right of way

ROADS AND PATHS

Not necessarily rights of way

M1 or A6(M)	Motorway
A 31(T)	Trunk or Main road
B 3074	Secondary road
A 35	Dual carriageway
	Road generally more than 4m wide
	Road generally less than 4m wide
··········	Other road, drive or track

Unfenced roads and tracks are shown by pecked lines

············   Path

RESOURCE 1.10b
OS map key.

RAILWAYS

——————   Multiple track } Standard
——————   Single track   } gauge
——————   Siding
——————   Narrow gauge
——————   Light Rapid Transit System
——————   Tunnel; cutting; embankment
——————   Road over; road under;
                level crossing

BOUNDARIES

As notified to October 1991

— · — · —   County (England and Wales),
                Region or Islands Area (Scotland)
— — — —   District
—·◇—·◇—   London Borough
·············   Civil Parish (England),
                Community (Wales)
— — — —   Constituency (County, Borough, Burgh
                or European Assembly)

SYMBOLS

↟	} Place	{ with tower
♁	of	with spire, minaret or dome
+	worship	without such additions
▫ ▭		Building; important building
▦ △		Glasshouse; youth hostel
⬭		Bus or coach station
⚓ ⚐		Lighthouse; beacon
△		Triangulation pillar
· T; A; R		Telephone: public; AA; RAC
▨▨▨		Sloping masonry
- - -□- - - -		Electricity transmission line
pylon pole		

○ W. Spr   Well, Spring
✛   Site of antiquity
✕ 1066   Site of battle (with date)
   Gravel pit
   Other pit or quarry
   Loose rock
   Outcrop
   Cliff

   Sand pit
   Refuse or slag heap
   Boulders
   Scree

[ ] Water   [ ] Mud
[ ] Sand; sand & shingle

NT	National Trust always open
NT	National Trust limited access, observe local signs
NTS NTS	National Trust for Scotland

VEGETATION

Limits of vegetation are defined by positioning of the symbols but may be delineated also by pecks or dots

↟↟ ↟↟   Coniferous trees
○ ○ ○   Non-coniferous trees
ᴵᴵ ᴵᴵ   Coppice

○ ○ ○ ○   Orchard
○-- --○--   Scrub
— —   Marsh, reeds, saltings.

Bracken, rough grassland
In some areas bracken (ꞁ) and rough
grassland (······) are shown separately
Heath
In some areas reeds (⌐) and saltings (⌐) are shown separately

Shown collectively
as rough grassland
on some sheets

HEIGHTS

| 50 · | Determined | { ground survey |
| 285 · | by | { air survey |

Surface heights are to the nearest metre above
mean sea level. Heights shown close to a
triangulation pillar refer to the ground level
height at the pillar and not necessarily at the summit

≈ 75
60
50

Contours are at
5 metres
vertical interval

---

7. a) Trace the map in Resource 1.9 which shows Leybourne in 1936.

b) Place your tracing over Leybourne on the Ordnance Survey map (Resource 1.10), which shows Leybourne in 1992.

c) Estimate the size of the built up area of Leybourne on each map. Choose from these numbers 0.1 km^2, 0.5 km^2, 0.8 km^2.

d) How much did Leybourne grow between 1936 and 1992?

e) Does the physical area of Leybourne make it an urban or rural settlement? Does the fact that it has joined on to nearby Larkfield and Lunsford make a difference?

1891

1991

Key

☐ Primary   ☐ Secondary

☐ Services

RESOURCE 1.11
Pie charts showing
employment type
in Leybourne.

Employment and Services

In the past, most people in rural areas worked in farming or other **primary industries**. People in urban areas mainly worked in factories (**secondary industry**) or **service industries** such as shops. For example in Leybourne in 1891, 49.5 per cent of people worked in farming and gardening, but no-one worked in a shop. Most people lived near their work. People often still think that work in rural areas is mainly connected with farming. However, today many people who work in factories or offices in urban areas may choose to live in the countryside and **commute** in to work in towns. This means that, as far as people's jobs go, many rural and urban areas are similar.

8. Look at Resource 1.11. How has employment in Leybourne changed from 1891 to 1991?

9. Can you think of any areas in Britain where most people aren't employed in service sector jobs?

RESOURCE 1.12
Services in Leybourne:
newsagents; printers;
hairdressers; and village hall.

RESOURCE 1.13a
Pub and restaurant.

Would you expect to find more things to do in a village or a city? A city normally has a greater variety and number of services such as shops or sports facilities. Some services, e.g. theatres tend only to be found in larger urban areas, whereas basic services such as public phones are found in most settlements. Urban areas usually have a good range of services.

10. Write a list of services you would expect to find in

a) a village

b) a town

11. Use the Ordnance Survey map (Resource 1.10) and the photos in Resources 1.12 and 1.13 to list the services available in Leybourne.

12. From the evidence you have collected from this page and the previous activities, is Leybourne a rural or urban settlement in terms of its employment and services?

RESOURCE 1.13b
Orchard which was cut
down to build the estate.

Is Leybourne rural or urban?

Before you decide, consider the views of these Leybourne residents . . .

Leybourne used to be a quiet countryside area until all the new estates were built in the 1980s — they covered over all the old fields and orchards and now we're part of one big area of housing. It means we have more shops, but it's not the same.

We've recently moved to Leybourne from London. It's much quieter here and it's only a few minutes walk to some pretty woods and fields. There's not as much to do here in the evenings, but it's less polluted and the motorway makes it easy to get to work.

Why do the two residents seem to be saying such different things about the same place?

You have looked at various aspects of Leybourne, now it's time to make the decision – is it rural or urban?

RESOURCE 1b
Leybourne Residents

13. Review the work you have done about Leybourne and fill in this table to summarise your findings. For each aspect tick whether you thought it showed that Leybourne was rural or urban.

Aspect of Leybourne	Urban	Rural
Population size		
Physical area		
People's jobs		
Services available		
Local people's views		

14. Overall, do you think Leybourne is a rural or urban settlement? Write a paragraph to explain your point of view.

15. Can you think of any other information that could have been useful to help you make your decision?

16. Is your own settlement rural or urban? Give reasons and evidence to explain. Does everyone in the class agree with your decision?

Why are there more people in some places than others?

RESOURCE 1.14
Aerial photo of Warkworth, Northumberland.

People are not usually spread evenly over an area, region or country. They tend to cluster together in villages, towns or cities. In the UK, 89 per cent of people live in urban areas, leaving only 11 per cent of people in rural areas.

Why do people cluster together in some places and not others? The sites of many present-day towns and cities reflect the needs of the first people who lived there. In the past, people were most concerned about their safety and getting a supply of food and water. Today, people want to be near employment and services such as schools.

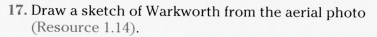

17. Draw a sketch of Warkworth from the aerial photo (Resource 1.14).

18. Label on your sketch the advantages of the site. Think about:

   - defence;
   - food and water supplies;
   - trade;
   - building houses;
   - communications – getting to other places.

19. Do you think these original advantages of the site are still important to people living in Warkworth today? Explain your answer.

20. For your own settlement, find out the location of the original site and why it was a good place for a settlement. How and why did it grow from the original site?

Although we don't need the castle to defend us any more, it's still useful because it brings in the tourists!

RESOURCE 1c
Warkworth Resident

How do settlement functions affect where people live?

Functions are the purposes of a settlement – what it provides for the people who live there. Functions such as defence that were important in the past are no longer so important today for settlements in most areas of the world. Some new functions such as the provision of education and leisure facilities are more important. However some functions such as shops and good communication links continue to be important.

From time to time, everyone needs the services that urban areas offer such as a library, department store or hospital. Many people choose to live in urban areas to be near to these services, whilst others choose to live in rural areas and travel into urban areas to use them. Some people have less choice over where they live than others.

Distribution means how something is spread across an area. Often a pattern can be seen, for example in Japan, most people live near the coast. There is usually a good reason for the distribution – in Japan it is mountainous inland. Resource 1.15 shows the distribution of people in Wales.

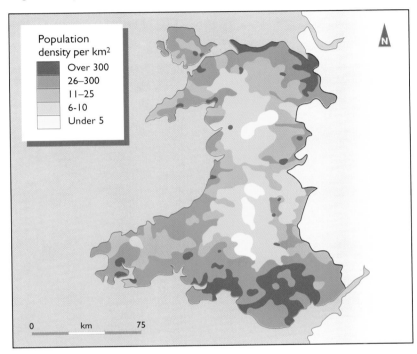

Population density per km²
- Over 300
- 26–300
- 11–25
- 6-10
- Under 5

0   km   75

RESOURCE 1.15
Population density in Wales.

To describe the **distribution** of something, you need to consider how it is spread out over the area:

- is it even or uneven?
- if it's uneven, is it **linear** (in lines), **clustered** (in clumps), or **random** (uneven, but no obvious pattern)? Sometimes there will be a mixture of patterns.
- Once you have identified the pattern(s), describe the important features e.g. 'the distribution shows a linear pattern along the coast'.

21. Describe the distribution of population in Wales. Use Resource 1.15 to help you. Try to explain the pattern.

How do physical factors affect population distribution?

Most of the decisions people make about where to live in the UK are based on **human** factors such as access to employment and services. However, in some countries, **physical** factors such as **relief** are more important.

The population distribution in Egypt is very uneven. Ninety nine per cent of the population live on just 4 per cent of the land area. This uneven distribution is caused by physical factors and the key is the River Nile. The satellite map (Resource 1.16a) will help you work out where people live and why.

RESOURCE 1.16a
Satellite map of River Nile, Egypt.

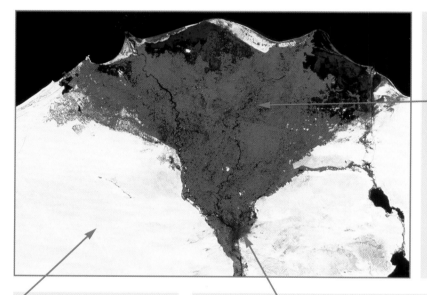

RESOURCE 1.16b Nile valley.

The Nile valley is a good area for farming. The land next to the river is flat and has fertile soil. The river provides water for **irrigation** (watering crops).

The land away from the river is desert. Very few plants grow here as it hardly ever rains.

Cairo is the capital of Egypt. It is located on the River Nile at the south of the Nile **delta**. It has good access to communication links and is in a strong position to govern the surrounding farmland.

RESOURCE 1.16c Cairo.

RESOURCE 1.16d
Desert in Egypt.

22. Describe and explain the location and distribution of urban areas in this part of Egypt.

23. Write a list of things your family might have thought about when deciding where to live. Are there more human or physical factors in your list? Compare your list with others in your class.

What is the world pattern of settlement?

Various factors make the distribution of the world's population very uneven. Some areas are popular to live in because they have a pleasant climate or there are lots of jobs, for example South East England. Some areas, such as Antarctica, are harder to live in because the climate is harsh, so fewer people live there. In some areas, the population is growing quickly, so they are becoming more crowded, whereas in other areas, people are moving away, so these areas become less densely populated.

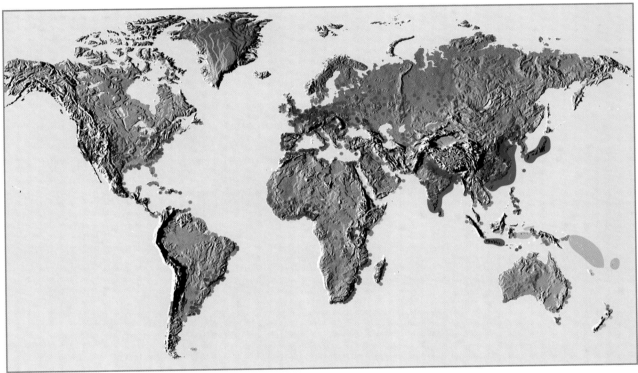

RESOURCE 1.17
World population distribution.

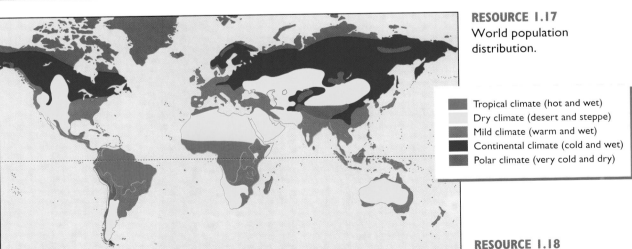

Tropical climate (hot and wet)
Dry climate (desert and steppe)
Mild climate (warm and wet)
Continental climate (cold and wet)
Polar climate (very cold and dry)

RESOURCE 1.18
World climate.

24. Use Resources 1.17 and 1.18 and your atlas to produce a report called 'Where in the world do people live?'. Your report should include:

- Where people are (Describe the distribution, using an atlas to help.)
- Why the distribution is like that (Think about physical factors e.g. relief, seas, rivers, climate and human factors e.g. making a living.)

ENQUIRY

Your task is to find out what a city is like, using resources available to you (for example library books or CD-ROM). Before you start, think about what you would like to find out about the city, and set yourself three or four enquiry questions to structure your research. You could present your findings as an information booklet for tourists, a wallchart or a short talk.

There are three key questions that will be important to your enquiry. Following each one are some suggestions for things that you might find out about. Try to limit your enquiry to look at just a few aspects of the city – otherwise you may take on a gigantic task!

Where is it? (location within the country with reference to other major settlements and physical features)
What is it like? (site, age, character, employment, built environment . . .)
Why is it like that? (growth, major historical events that influenced it, government involvement, trade and industry links . . .)

EVALUATING SETTLEMENTS

Key Idea

The way we perceive, and form opinions, of settlements depends not only on the characteristics of the settlement and what we have seen or heard about it, but also our individual, personal values. These values differ widely from one person to another depending greatly on their situation, but are there country-wide perceptions on what constitutes a good quality of living?

What image do people have of Cambridge?

What is distinctive about Cambridge?

> Cambridge is a small city in East Anglia with a population of 117 000. It is an old city, well-known for its university, and many famous people such as Sir Isaac Newton and Charles Darwin have lived here.

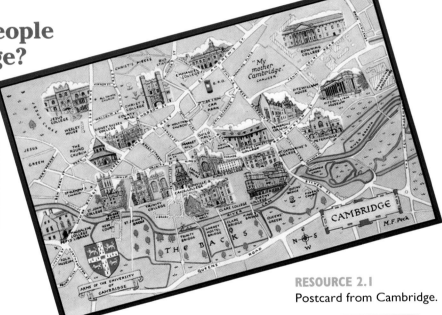

RESOURCE 2.1
Postcard from Cambridge.

> We get thousands of tourists from all over the world coming to Cambridge each year to see the beautiful buildings and to go punting on the River Cam. You can see all the important places on this post card (Resource 2.1).

Refer to the postcard (Resource 2.1) to answer these questions:

1. What types of places are shown on the postcard?

2. Why do you think the postcard designer chose these places?

3. What other sorts of buildings are likely to be in a town centre, which are not shown on the postcard?

4. Why do you think these places have been omitted?

5. Does it matter that the post card only shows one aspect of Cambridge?

Of course, a tourist visiting Cambridge would see more than just what was on this postcard, so would have more information about the character of the city, but do you think they would see everything? After all, Cambridge does cover 34 km²! A tourist visiting Cambridge, leaves with a particular view or **image** of what it is like. Everyone has their own image of a place, even if they have not visited the place, but have just heard about it from other people or seen it on the television.

RESOURCE 2.2

A mental map of Cambridge.

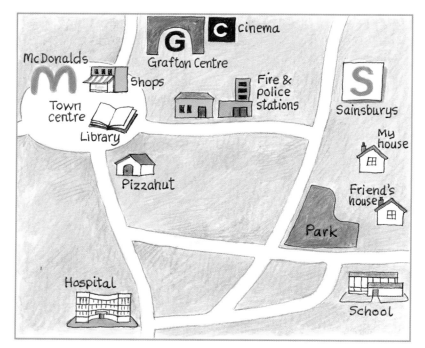

Tourists aren't the only people who have an image of a city. Other groups such as local business people, or school children, will have a different view of what the city is like. People who know the city fairly well will remember how to get to all the places that are important to them. They have a **mental map** of part of the city. Someone who has lived in Cambridge for a long time is likely to have a more detailed mental map of it than someone who is just visiting for the day. The map below (Resource 2.2) is a combination of mental maps drawn by some Year 7 pupils in Cambridge. It shows the places in the town that are important to them and their life in Cambridge.

6. Compare the pupil's map with the postcard map. Find four things that are different.

7. Why do you think that the two maps are so different?

8. Which one of the images of Cambridge is more realistic? Give reasons to explain why.

Most settlements have many different aspects to them, some positive and some negative. The positive features are often publicised by settlements to attract people to the area. The images we have of places are important because we use them to make decisions that may affect ourselves and others. For example, if a tourist came away from Cambridge with a positive image of the city, they may want to visit again, do business in the area or even consider living there in the future. Sometimes an exaggerated or inaccurate image of a place is held by many people. This is called a stereotype.

9. If a person had not visited Cambridge, could they still have an image of the city? If so, where would the image come from?

10. What is a stereotype? Why can it sometimes be unhelpful for people to have a stereotyped image of a place?

What types of settlement do you like?

The character of the place where someone lives or works will affect their life – some people will enjoy living or working in a busy city, whilst others prefer to live in a quiet, rural area. It is quite hard to measure how much someone likes the place where they live. One method is called **bipolar analysis** (Resource 2.3).

USING THE BIPOLAR ANALYSIS TABLE

- Looking at just one photo, work through each row of the table. If the feature of the photo is good, it is given a positive score, if it is bad, it is given a negative score.

- Multiply the number of ticks in a column by the number at the top of the column to give each column total.

- Add up the column totals to give the grand total (see example in Resource 2.4).

- The more positive the score, the more you liked the photo. The highest possible score would be +10 and the lowest possible would be −10.

- Preferences vary from person to person, so don't be surprised if your friends' scores are different from your own.

	+2	+1	0	−1	−2	
Attractive						Unattractive
Interesting						Uninteresting
Welcoming						Threatening
A good amount of people						Too busy or too quiet
A good amount of buildings						Too many/few buildings
Column totals:						Grand total: /10

RESOURCE 2.3
Bipolar analysis table.

	+2	+1	0	−1	−2	
Attractive	✓					Unattractive
Interesting		✓				Uninteresting
Welcoming			✓			Threatening
A good amount of people	✓					Too busy or too quiet
A good amount of buildings				✓		Too many/few buildings
Column totals:	+4	+1	0	−1	0	Grand total: 4/10

RESOURCE 2.4
Example of scoring.

In bipolar analysis, you give a place a score for different aspects of its character. The score can then be used to compare your reactions to different places.

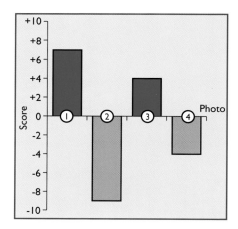

RESOURCE 2.5
Example of a graph showing results of bipolar analysis.

11. Complete a bipolar analysis for each of the photos below. You could use three different tables, or three different colours on a large copy of the table.

12. Choose one of the photos and explain why you gave it this score.

13. Draw a bar graph to compare the three scores. If some of your scores are negative, you will need a negative axis on your graph (see Resource 2.5).

14. Compare your scores with other people in your class. Overall did people in your class prefer the urban or rural photos? Why do you think this was?

RESOURCE 2.5a
Desert settlement.

RESOURCE 2.5b
Living in a large city.

RESOURCE 2.5c
Life in the mountains.

What is Quality of Life and how does it vary between countries?

Quality of life is how satisfied someone is with their living conditions and lifestyle. Quality of life is quite hard to measure because some people are happy with circumstances which other people would find unbearable.

THE DE GOESE FAMILY
Location: São Paulo, Brazil
Household size: 6
Size of house: 103 m^2
Working week: 50 hours (father); 'constant' (mother)
Consumer goods: Radio, television, VCR, car
% Income spent on food: 55
Wishes for future: Better car, better stereo, better home.

RESOURCE 2.6
De Goese family.

THE GETU FAMILY
Location: Rural Ethiopia
Household size: 7
Size of house: 30 m^2
Working week: 80 hours (father); 126 hours (mother)
Consumer goods: Radio
% Income spent on food: grow own
Wishes for future: More animals, second set of clothes, peace

RESOURCE 2.7
Getu family.

THE ABDULLA FAMILY
Location: Kuwait City, Kuwait
Household size: 7
Size of house: 450 m^2
Working week: 50 hours (father)
Consumer goods: 4 radios, 2 televisions, 2 VCRs, 4 cars
% Income spent on food: 29
Wishes for the future: Fishing boat, more income and leisure time for holidays

RESOURCE 2.8
Abdulla family.

15. Use the information from this page and your own views to write a list of factors which can affect someone's quality of life.

16. Write a factfile about your own family's quality of life in the same format as the ones above. Include a drawing or photo.

17. Put the four families (including your own) in order from highest to lowest quality of life. Explain why you put them in this order.

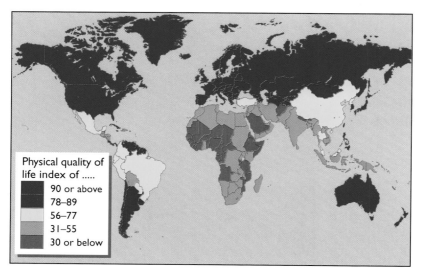

RESOURCE 2.9

Map showing physical quality of life index.

Some factors that affect quality of life such as income and the standard of healthcare are easier to measure. In this section we will see big differences in quality of life between different countries, and even within different areas of the same country.

Not all the families within these three countries will be the same as our examples, but they do illustrate some general differences around the world – people in some areas have a much better quality of life than people in other areas. The Overseas Development Council have developed a way of combining three important aspects of quality of life to give a 'score' for each of the countries of the world. They call this the **Physical Quality of Life Index**. They include **literacy** (per cent of the population who can read), life expectancy (the average amount of years people live) and **infant mortality** (the proportion of babies who die before their first birthday). The higher the score in the index the better the quality of life in the country. The map in Resource 2.9 shows the results for the Physical Quality of Life Index.

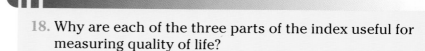

18. Why are each of the three parts of the index useful for measuring quality of life?

19. Using an atlas and Resource 2.9, name three countries in the world which score well on the Index and three which score badly.

20. Describe any general patterns you can see on the map. Do people in some continents generally have a better quality of life than others? Is there a difference between North and South?

21. Find Brazil, Ethiopia, Kuwait and the UK on the Physical Quality of Life Index map. Write down the 'score' for each one. Do the families that you wrote about in question 3 have the quality of life that you would expect in those countries?

22. The United Nations estimates that these 8 cities will be the largest in the world in the year 2000:

    ☐ Mexico City   ☐ Tokyo   ☐ Bombay   ☐ Seoul
    ☐ Sao Paulo   ☐ Calcutta   ☐ New York   ☐ Tehran

    Use your atlas to plot the cities on a world map. Look back to Resource 2.9 to say what the quality of life is likely to be like in these cities. Is this situation acceptable?

How does Quality of Life vary within a country?

From the Physical Quality of Life Index (Resource 2.9), we saw that the average quality of life varied a lot between countries. However, the situation is really much more complex than these averages suggest. All countries have areas where quality of life is better and worse than the average.

People sometimes refer to a 'North–South Divide' in Britain. This is shown in Resource 2.10. The South of Britain is felt to have a better quality of life than the north. When you look at statistics such as average earnings, the average person is certainly more wealthy in the South, however, some costs of living, such as house prices are also higher. As we have seen in the previous section, factors such as quality of environment and relationships with others also affect quality of life. Do these follow a North–South divide too? In reality, patterns of quality of life are probably even more complex than the North–South pattern suggests.

RESOURCE 2.10
North–South divide in the UK.

North–South Divide still with us!

Recent reports show that it is still much better to live in the South of Britain than the North. Average weekly pay for men in Greater London in 1995 was £498.20 compared to just £331.70 in Northern England. Wages are also rising faster in the South than in the North. Unemployment rates in 1995 varied from 6.2 per cent in East Anglia to 10.6 per cent in Northern England, whilst Scotland was slightly lower at 8.2 per cent and Wales at 8.5 per cent. These figures must affect how much people can spend – for example 25 per cent of people in the South East own a dishwasher, compared to 13 per cent in Yorkshire and Humberside. On the other hand, the North West has the highest ownership of microwave ovens (67 per cent), compared to 57 per cent in Greater London, so maybe the picture isn't quite so clear after all!

23. From the newspaper article, what evidence can you find that a North–South divide exists?

24. Do you agree that 'it is much better to live in the South of Britain than the North'?

25. Can you think of any places that are exceptions to the North–South quality of life pattern?

26. Why might planners and decision-makers be interested in information about a North–South divide?

A team of researchers at Glasgow University put the largest 38 cities in Britain in order from best to worst quality of life. They worked this out by asking people what was most important to their quality of life. Some of the most important things turned out to be low crime rates, good health facilities, low rates of pollution, a low cost of living, good shops and a lack of racism. The 'top' fifteen towns they identified are shown in Resource 2.11.

RESOURCE 2.11

Top fifteen towns and cities to live in in Britain.

1. Edinburgh
2. Aberdeen
3. Plymouth
4. Cardiff
5. Hamilton–Motherwell
6. Bradford
7. Reading
8. Stoke-on-Trent
9. Middlesborough
10. Sheffield
11. Oxford
12. Leicester
13. Brighton
14. Portsmouth
15. Southampton

27. Use your atlas to find out where these towns are. How many of them are in the 'North' as shown on Resource 2.10? Can you work out the percentage figure?

28. Were you surprised that any of the top 15 towns were in the list? If so, explain why.

29. If the survey had been broadened to include rural areas as well, do you think the results would have been different? Explain why/why not.

ENQUIRY

In your class, split into small groups. Each group should take one of the top 15 towns and cities and find out about it from books, tourist brochures or the Internet. You should aim to find a good photo or drawing which you feel is typical of the area, write a fact file giving key information such as population figures, and a short description of what you think the advantages and disadvantages of living there would be. You could report back to your class in an oral presentation, or combine your work to produce a wall display. To conclude, you could discuss whether you agree with the Glasgow University researchers on the order of the cities as regards quality of life.

An inadequate quality of life? Homelessness in Britain

'Homelessness' often makes us think of people sleeping on the streets, but actually this is just the tip of the iceberg. A person can still be homeless even if they have a roof over their heads – for example they could be staying in a hostel or staying with friends because they have nowhere else to go (Resource 2.12). It is hard to obtain accurate figures on homelessness, but one estimate in 1990 put the number of homeless people at 2 million in the UK as a whole, whilst another estimated there were 64 500 homeless people in London alone. Lack of affordable housing is a problem in rural areas as well as in towns and cities.

The table (Resource 2.13) shows some reasons why people became homeless in 1993. Do you find any of the reasons or figures surprising?

RESOURCE 2.13
Reasons for homelessness.

Reason	% people
Parents, relatives or friends are no longer willing/able to house the person	40
Break up of relationship with partner	18
Loss of rented home (various reasons) or loss of home connected with previous job	17
Other reasons e.g. refugee	15
Unable to continue paying for home (mortgage or rent arrears)	10

Without a home, it is hard to get a job because employers are often put off applicants who cannot give their address. This means it is hard to get money and to find somewhere permanent to live again. Many people stay with friends or 'squat' in unoccupied houses to avoid having to sleep in the streets. Sleeping rough is a last resort because it is dangerous and unhealthy – in 1989, 375 people died from hypothermia (getting too cold) on the streets of England and Wales.

Much work to help improve quality of life for homeless people is done by national charities, such as Shelter, or more local groups. This work may receive funding from local councils or national government. Housing projects include nightshelters and support to find longer term accommodation, whilst organisations such as the 'Big Issue' magazine employ homeless people. It is hard to get everyone to the point at which they can afford, and cope with, private rented housing, and many people are not eligible for council housing.

30. Draw a pie chart to show the causes of homelessness. Can you think of any more situations that would fit in the 'other' category?

31. Is it true that anyone can become homeless?

32. Who should deal with the problem of homelessness? Is there anything you could do?

RESOURCE 2.14
Equalville.

How does Quality of Life vary within settlements?

Welcome to Equalville! Five hundred families live here, each with four members. We all live in three-bedroom, semi-detached houses built in 1940. All the families earn enough for their needs and each has one car and two televisions.

Although each settlement is different, towns and cities in More Economically Developed Countries (MEDCs) often have similar areas. The map (Resource 2.15) shows some of these typical areas.

RESOURCE 2.15
Typical land use pattern in an MEDC city.

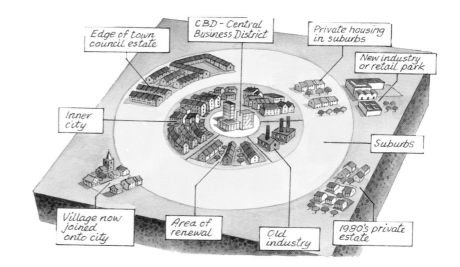

33. What would be the advantages and disadvantages of living in somewhere like Equalville (Resource 2.14)?

34. Why do you think Equalville is unlikely to exist?

35. Work with a partner to produce a list of differences you would usually find within a settlement.

36. Make a large copy of the map and colour in areas according to how good you think quality of life would be. Use these classes:

   ▢ Above average   ▢ Average   ▢ Below average

37. What general pattern can you see on the map?

38. Can you think of any areas in a town or city you know that fit in with the pattern shown on the map?

39. What factors influence which area of the town someone lives in?

Towns and cities within Less Economically Developed Countries (LEDCs) also have areas where quality of life is good and areas where it is poor. In fact the difference between rich and poor is much more noticeable than it is in MEDCs.

In Lima, the capital of Peru, many of the low quality housing areas are found on the outskirts of the city. This is because they are relatively new areas. Settlements such as Comas (Resource 2.16) consist of shacks that people have built for themselves. The building land is poor and to start with there is no piped water, sewage or electricity. People have to travel a long way into the town centre to work. Hours are long and pay is unreliable. Children often have to travel a long way to school, and may not be able to carry on into further education because they are needed to earn a wage. Older areas of low income housing can be found towards the city centre where old houses have been divided up into rooms that people can rent. These usually have better services, but are in a poor state of repair and it is sometimes hard for people to keep up with the rent payments.

RESOURCE 2.16
Lima, Peru.

By contrast, the richer areas of Lima, such as San Isidro (Resource 2.16), have luxury flats and big villas with gardens. The rich earn good incomes in stable jobs in the city centre and usually have a number of maids to take care of the household tasks. This leaves leisure time to enjoy sports and social facilities. The children from these areas are usually educated in private schools and are likely to get good jobs in their turn, continuing their good quality of life.

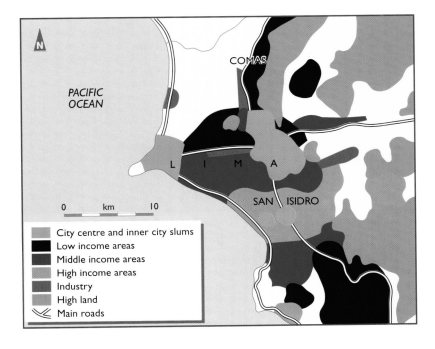

City centre and inner city slums
Low income areas
Middle income areas
High income areas
Industry
High land
Main roads

41. Using the map (Resource 2.16), describe the location of

   a) the high-income areas

   b) the newer low income areas.

   Suggest some reasons why they are in these locations.

42. How is the pattern of high and low income areas in Lima different to the pattern you would expect in a British city?

An Inadequate Quality of Life? Squatter Settlements in Manila, Philippines

Manila is the capital of the Philippines in South East Asia. The rich enjoy an excellent quality of life, but the population of the city has grown very fast, and many people are very poor – in 1988, the average family income was US$91 per month. If people cannot afford to buy or rent a house of reasonable quality, they end up sharing with friends or relatives, often leading to very overcrowded conditions. The people who cannot share have no choice but to build their own makeshift house in any areas where there is space. These areas are called **squatter settlements** or **shanty towns** (Resource 2. 17). Over 3.5 million people live in slums in the Manila area.

Shanty towns are often illegally built on someone else's land, so the residents may be in constant danger of eviction. Houses are likely to be poor quality because people cannot afford permanent building materials, though they may make improvements to their house over time. Few areas have proper services such as sewage, running water and electricity.

RESOURCE 2.17
A house in a shanty town.

In many cities in LEDCs, the squatter settlements are on the outskirts of town, where there is more space, but in Manila, they are scattered throughout the urban areas on land that no-one else wants, such as rubbish dumps and railway sidings (Resource 2.18). One example of a squatter settlement in Manila is 'Pobres Park' where 10 000 families live. The area is controlled by a local group, who charge rent to the occupants. There is no piped water – instead it is supplied by water sellers – and electricity is provided by illegally hooking into a nearby building.

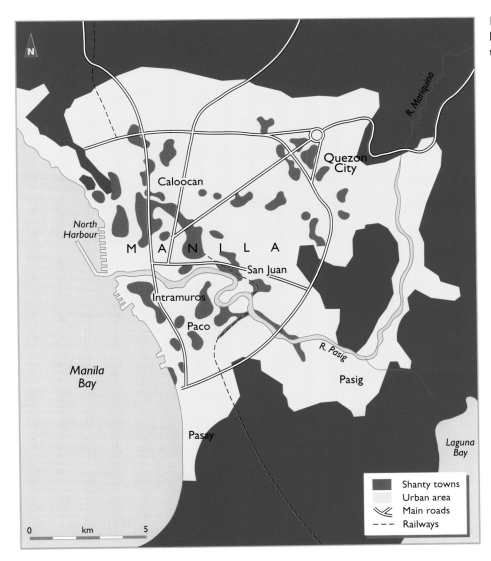

Distribution of shanty towns in Manila.

Many people in squatter settlements work in **informal** services such as street trading. In Manila, until 1995, around 20 000 people lived on a massive rubbish dump called 'Smoky Mountain'. They earned money by sorting through the rubbish to extract items to recycle. Now the area has been sold and is going to be turned into a commercial reprocessing plant. Part of the profits are to be spent on a new housing scheme, but in 1997 those who accepted a place in it were still in a temporary camp. The families who refused to leave Smoky Mountain were violently evicted.

43. Draw a sketch of the shanty house in Resource 2.17 and annotate it to show the main aspects of living in a shanty town.

44. Describe the distribution of shanty towns in Resource 2.18

SERVICING SETTLEMENTS

> ## Key Idea
>
> The provision of services in a settlement can be anything from a telephone box on the corner to a large shopping centre and a ten screen cinema on the high street, or a small clinic open two days a week to a large sixth form studies centre. There is a cycle to services: the amount of people in the area who will use the services usually determines what will be supplied; and the services supplied often determine whether people will move into, or out of, an area.

What types of services are there in settlements?

Some people have a job which provides a service to people or organisations. Service jobs are also referred to as tertiary industry. Services include retail (shops), education, emergency services, finance and tourism. Within each of these, there are many different jobs, for example healthcare includes jobs in hospitals as well as in local doctors' surgeries. Some services are more specialised than others. This means they concentrate on providing one aspect of the service, for example an opticians. Other services are less specialised, for example a department store which sells many different types of goods.

1. List 20 different services, giving examples from the different groups such as education, healthcare and retail.

2. From the point of view of your family, put your list in order with the least frequently used services at the top and the most frequently used at the bottom.

3. Which of the services are specialised and which are more general? Colour code your list to show which are which.

4. Is there any relationship between how specialised a service is and how frequently it is used?

More specialised services tend to be used less frequently by individual people, so they are usually located in towns or cities where there are more people and more potential customers so that many people can use them. People are willing to travel further to go to specialist shops such as a jewellers or travel agent than to a newsagents or bakers. It would be hard for a jewellers to make a profit if it was located in a small village in a rural area, but a general store would be able to get enough customers to survive.

Across a whole country, there are a lot of villages with a small number of general services in each one, and a smaller number of cities with a large number of both specialised and general services in each. This pattern is called a hierarchy (see Resource 3.1).

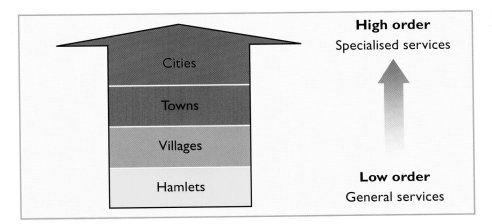

RESOURCE 3.1
The service hierarchy.

5. Which of the services on your list would you expect to find in a small village? Which would you expect to find in a large town? Which place would have more services? Give reasons to explain the differences.

6. Make a large copy of the diagram (Resource 3.1) and add the following labels:

   Lots of people nearby; Few people nearby; People willing to travel a long way to visit the services; People will only travel a short distance to visit the services.

7. Give an example of the services you might expect to find at each level of the hierarchy for each of the following groups of services:

   a) education

   b) healthcare

   For example, sports facilities might vary from a single tennis court at the village level, to a small swimming pool at the town level, to a full sports centre with skating rink at the city level.

How does service provision vary in the Isle of Skye?

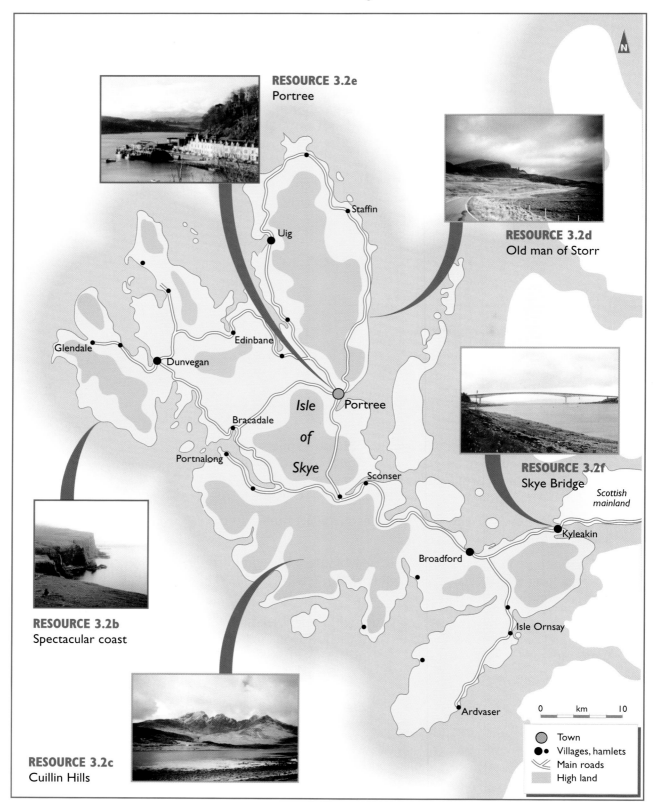

RESOURCE 3.2e
Portree

RESOURCE 3.2d
Old man of Storr

Staffin

Uig

Edinbane

Glendale

Dunvegan

Isle
of
Skye

Portree

Bracadale

Portnalong

Sconser

RESOURCE 3.2f
Skye Bridge

Scottish
mainland

Kyleakin

Broadford

Isle Ornsay

RESOURCE 3.2b
Spectacular coast

Ardvaser

0   km   10

Town
Villages, hamlets
Main roads
High land

RESOURCE 3.2c
Cuillin Hills

Skye is a large island off the North West coast of Scotland. There is a population of 8500, mostly living in many small villages and hamlets scattered around the island (Resource 3.2). The main town of Portree and many of the villages are located near the coast so that people could fish, and because the island is very hilly inland, making building hard. In the past, most people had small, self sufficient farms (crofts), but now tourism is an increasingly important industry.

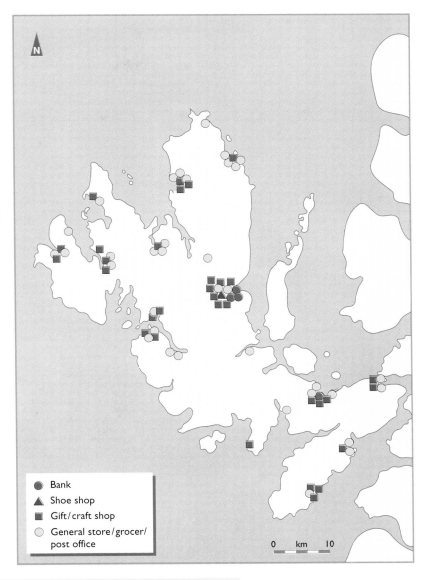

● Bank
▲ Shoe shop
■ Gift/craft shop
○ General store/grocer/ post office

0   km   10

RESOURCE 3.3
Selected services on Skye

The map above (Resource 3.3) shows the distribution of four services on Skye.

Use the map and the knowledge you have gained so far in this section to answer the following questions:

8. List how many of each type of service are shown on the map.

9. Explain why there are more general stores (Resource 3.4) than shoe shops. Think about frequency of use, distance customers are prepared to travel and size of **market** needed.

10. Can you explain why there are so many gift/craft shops on the island when these are a fairly specialised service?

11. Put the 13 labelled settlements on Resource 3.2 into order according to the number and range of services they offer.

EDUCATION

Although there are 17 junior schools on the island, there is only one senior school, located at Portree. As this would mean a long journey for children living in more remote areas of Skye, it is possible to stay in boarding houses in Portree during the week and just go home for the weekend.

SPECIALIST GOODS

Many specialist shops, including high street 'brand name' clothing stores such as Top Shop are not available on the island at all. This means that many people regularly make the $2\frac{1}{2}$ hour journey over mountain roads to Inverness to shop for high order goods. Larger articles may have to be delivered by lorry from Inverness or Glasgow, incurring further expense. The bridge to the mainland from Kyleakin has made the journey quicker, but tolls have to be paid.

RESOURCE 3.4a
Mobile vets, Isle of Skye.

TRAVELLING TO SERVICES

Travelling by car through Skye has been made easier by a road improvement programme funded by the European Union (EU) and Highlands and Islands Development Board, but many roads are still single track with passing places. Roads can rarely take a straight line between villages due to the need to avoid mountains and lochs. In Winter, snow can slow down journeys and block the road to Inverness. Access to services in remote areas is improved by mobile services such as a library van or mobile vets (see Resource 3.4). Mail order is becoming increasingly popular, especially for clothes.

RESOURCE 3.4b
General stores, Kyleakin.

ENQUIRY

Use the three pages about services in Skye to work through these questions:

12. Describe the level of service provision on Skye. Mention range and number of services, as well as ease of access from different areas of the island and for different groups of the population such as elderly people.

13. Evaluate the level of provision. Is it appropriate for the population?

14. Compare the level of provision in Skye with your local area.

15. Recommend any changes to the level of provision or access to services in Skye.

What is service provision like in urban areas?

Urban areas usually have a better provision of services than rural areas – they have more high order services and more choice for the inhabitants. However, within a city, not everyone has equal access to all the services. Up to the 1960s in Britain, the major shopping area was located in the city centre, with corner shops providing low order goods for the inner city and some rows of shops located on main roads into the city (see Resource 3.5). However, more recently, there has been a trend to build shopping centres and superstores on out-of-town sites, for example the Metrocentre, Gateshead (Resource 3.6).

RESOURCE 3.5
Shopping areas in a typical city.

Out of town sites are sometimes favoured by shops over city centre ones because they have:

- better access for cars, a popular method of travelling to shops avoiding city centre parking problems and congestion and on-site car parks;

- more space for larger stores mean that goods such as food can be bought in bulk;

- cheaper land and space for large buildings.

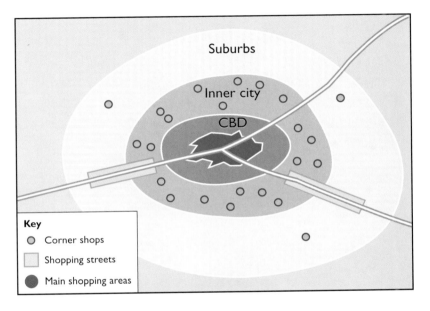

Key
- ○ Corner shops
- ☐ Shopping streets
- ● Main shopping areas

RESOURCE 3.6
Metrocentre, Gateshead.

Building shops on green belt land on the outskirts of cities is usually controversial as it removes open space used as farmland or for recreation. Although the new shops please people with cars, not everyone may benefit as independent shops in the town centre such as butchers may be unable to cope with the competition from new supermarkets on the edge of town. This would reduce choice for those without a car who find it difficult to use the new facilities.

RESOURCE 3.7
Possible locations for a supermarket.

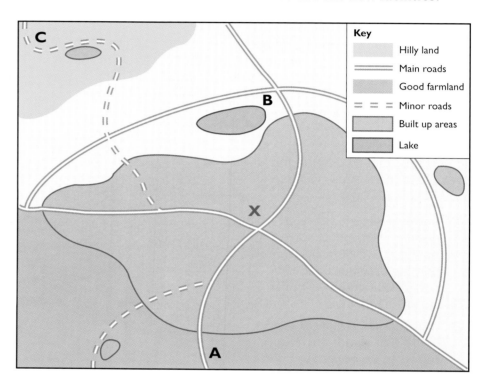

16. A supermarket wants to move from site X to a new site (Resource 3.7). It is considering sites A, B and C. You have been asked to advise them on the best site.

a) Make a table of advantages and disadvantages of each of the four sites (A, B, C and X).

b) Which new site would you recommend to the supermarket? Explain your decision.

c) Explain how your choice might affect:

i. shops in the city centre
ii. a student on a low income, without a car, living in the inner city
iii. an elderly couple with a car living in the suburbs.

d) Are there any ways in which you could reduce the disadvantages of your chosen site to make it even more attractive?

MOVING ON

4

Key Idea

People move from one area to another for many different reasons. Some moves are temporary – perhaps to study abroad or to find better grazing land for cattle, whilst others are more permanent. If a person moves home with the intention of staying at their new location, it is called migration. When people move out of a country it is called emigration and when they move into a country it is called immigration.

Why do people move?

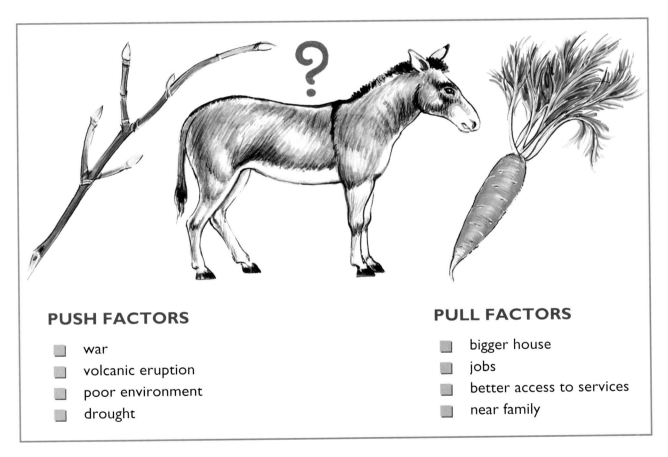

PUSH FACTORS

- war
- volcanic eruption
- poor environment
- drought

PULL FACTORS

- bigger house
- jobs
- better access to services
- near family

The decision to move is often complicated. There are usually reasons why the person wants to move away from the old area (**push factors**) and reasons why they want to move to the new area (**pull factors**), see Resource 4.1. People usually migrate because they think their quality of life will improve, but this does not always happen.

RESOURCE 4.1
Why do people move?

Sometimes people have no choice but to move because their home is in danger from natural hazards, such as volcanic eruption, or war. People who are forced to move away from their homes are called **refugees**. If many people move into or out of a country, its population size will be affected, which may cause problems for the local people and government of the country into which they move, as housing and food will have to be provided until the refugees can move back.

Transport links have improved a lot over the last century, making it easier for people to move to new areas or countries. However it is still not possible for everyone to live anywhere they like in the world because the costs of moving may be too high, and some countries have strict controls on immigration.

1. Explain why a donkey, carrot and stick are used in Resource 4.1 to show the push and pull factors involved in migration.

2. Write down five more examples of push factors and five more pull factors.

3. Imagine you could move anywhere you wanted to in the world. Where would you go? What push and pull factors are involved in your decision to move?

4. Why do you think that many countries control immigration? Do you think this should happen?

Why move to Cape Town?

Cape Town was founded around 300 years ago and became an important centre for international trade. Many Europeans emigrated to South Africa and settled in Cape Town to make money through importing and exporting goods. This increased the size of the country's population. People still move from Europe to Cape Town because there are opportunities for a good quality of life there, as long as the migrant can afford it.

The largest number of people arriving in Cape Town are from within South Africa itself. They move from areas in the surrounding countryside to find jobs and education for their families. Moving from the countryside to the city is called **rural-to-urban migration** Under the apartheid system, before the present government was elected, migration to Cape Town for black people was tightly controlled – you could only move if you had a job. Now the laws are more relaxed, so many people have moved to the city from rural areas in the East Cape. A lot of the migrants have to live in shanty towns because there is not enough low cost permanent housing in the city.

Sometimes migrants are attracted by the 'bright lights' of the city (the idea that everything they want will be available to them), but their expectations aren't always fulfilled.

Frank and Marion Ullman moved to central Cape Town from Munich, Germany.

I love the views from our house and I have a lot of opportunities now for all my sports — golf, tennis and surfing. I have a successful business here making PVC windows, so it's fantastic for me — I love it very much.

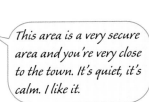

This area is a very secure area and you're very close to the town. It's quiet, it's calm. I like it.

Bongi and her family moved here from the rural East Cape and now live in a squatter settlement at Philippi, 20 km from the town centre.

My mother came here 15 years ago because she couldn't make a living as a farmer due to the droughts. She wants us to be educated, so we will have a better chance in life and be able to earn more money. I don't want to go back to the countryside — it's no fun at all. You have to fetch water from very far away. I hate the idea of carrying a bucket of water on my head — that's just not right. Some people I know worry about the crime in Cape Town, and prefer the community in the countryside — they don't forget our roots.

5. Make a list of push and pull factors in the move to Cape Town for

   a) Frank and Marion Ullman

   b) Bongi and her family.

6. Which family do you think has the best quality of life in Cape Town? Give reasons to explain your choice.

7. Which family do you think has gained the most from the move? Why?

8. Why do you think that not everyone in the rural area has moved to Cape Town?

9. Can you think of any other reasons why people might not be able to migrate?

Refugees – the case of Rwanda

In 1995 there were an estimated 27 million refugees in the world. Particularly large numbers of refugees left countries such as Palestine, Afghanistan, Rwanda and the former Yugoslavia because their safety was threatened by war or persecution. These numbers of people moving may raise or lower the population of neighbouring countries by up to 2 or 3 million people. This may strain the host country's resources in providing food and shelter for the refugees and cause unrest amongst the local population.

Rwanda is a country slightly larger than Wales situated in the mountainous Eastern Central area of Africa. The population was 7.9 million in 1995 with only 6 per cent of people living in urban areas. Most people in the rural area are subsistence farmers growing crops such as beans and bananas. Rwanda has a history of struggle between the two main **ethnic groups** called the Hutus and Tutsis. The latest conflict began in 1990 and rose to a crisis when in 1994 a **civil war** began and more than 500 000 Rwandans were killed in three months. Half of the population were forced away from their homes and an estimated 2.4 million fled to nearby countries (Resource 4.2). These massive movements of people had a significant effect, not only on the refugees, but on the population of neighbouring countries.

RESOURCE 4.2

Map of migration in Rwanda and surrounding area.

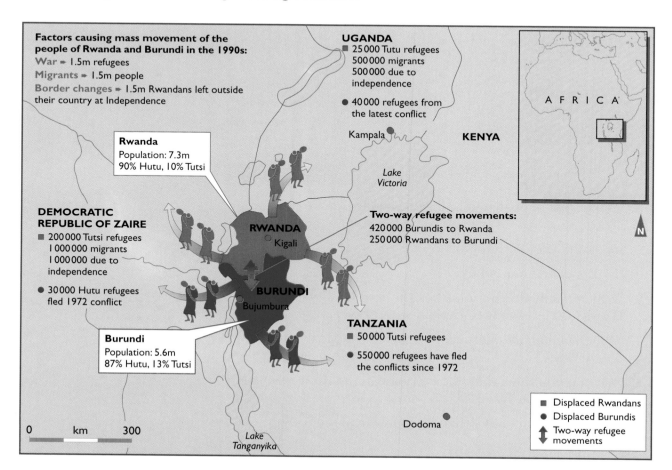

Factors causing mass movement of the people of Rwanda and Burundi in the 1990s:
War ➡ 1.5m refugees
Migrants ➡ 1.5m people
Border changes ➡ 1.5m Rwandans left outside their country at Independence

Rwanda
Population: 7.3m
90% Hutu, 10% Tutsi

UGANDA
■ 25 000 Tutu refugees
500 000 migrants
500 000 due to independence
● 40 000 refugees from the latest conflict

Kampala

KENYA

Lake Victoria

A F R I C A

DEMOCRATIC REPUBLIC OF ZAIRE
■ 200 000 Tutsi refugees
1 000 000 migrants
1 000 000 due to independence
● 30 000 Hutu refugees fled 1972 conflict

RWANDA
Kigali

Two-way refugee movements:
420 000 Burundis to Rwanda
250 000 Rwandans to Burundi

BURUNDI
Bujumbura

Burundi
Population: 5.6m
87% Hutu, 13% Tutsi

TANZANIA
■ 50 000 Tutsi refugees
● 550 000 refugees have fled the conflicts since 1972

Dodoma

N

0   km   300

Lake Tanganyika

■ Displaced Rwandans
● Displaced Burundis
↕ Two-way refugee movements

The United Nations High Commission for Refugees (UNHCR) set up and managed refugee camps for those forced to flee. Two billion dollars was spent on refugee relief at the beginning of the crisis alone. So many refugees needed help that camps became overcrowded (Resource 4.5), which made it easy for diseases like cholera to spread amongst people already weakened by their long journey and the terrible events they had lived through. Many children had become separated from their families during the fighting or on the journey. At one camp in Zaire, conditions were made worse because people had to chop down the surrounding trees for firewood, which caused soil erosion in heavy rain. It was impossible to grow crops in the remaining soil, so food shortages were common. The countries that the refugees had moved to found it hard to contribute to the refugees' well-being as their resources were limited.

Since 1996, many refugees have been returning to Rwanda, partly because they wish to return to their homes and partly due to events such as civil war in eastern Zaire which have forced them to move away. However, many people returned to their homes to find that their crops and stores of food had been destroyed by troops or eaten by refugees passing through. There was little paid work available and it was hard to get money to plant new crops. Since 1994, the UNHCR has been helping people in Rwanda to rebuild their houses and facilities and care for unaccompanied children.

RESOURCE 4.3
Refugee camp for Rwandan refugees.

10. From the map in Resource 4.2, which countries received the most refugees from Rwanda and Burundi? Why did the refugees choose these countries?

11. Draw a large outline map of the countries in 4.4. Draw on the arrows showing the flows of refugees, making the width of the arrows proportional to the numbers of refugees. Add on the flows between Rwanda and Burundi. Describe the pattern your map shows.

12. What problems do refugees face?

13. You are a representative for UNHCR. What action do you need to take to help the refugees immediately and later to help them return to Rwanda?

Why do some settlements grow?

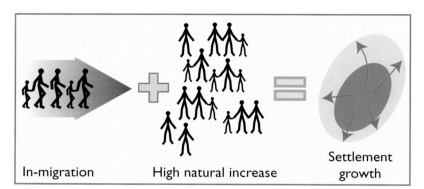

In-migration   High natural increase   Settlement growth

RESOURCE 4.4
The causes of settlement

Settlement growth can be seen in two ways – a higher population and a larger amount of space being taken up by the city.

There are two reasons why a settlement grows (Resource 4.4). Firstly people may migrate to the settlement – this is called **in-migration**.

In most countries, this movement is usually from rural areas to urban areas, as in Cape Town. Secondly there may also be a **natural increase** of the population. This is because more babies are being born than people are dying. This often happens at the same time as rural-to-urban migration because many of the people moving from the rural areas to urban areas are fairly young, and tend to bring children with them or start families once they arrive resulting in a high **birth rate**. Settlements therefore increase in population and area.

As the population grows, there is a need for more housing, so the settlement spreads outward. In LEDCs, this outward city growth is often rapid and unplanned, leading to large areas of shanty towns, such as those on the Cape Flats in Cape Town. The populations of most richer cities are no longer growing rapidly, though the city may still be spreading outwards. Instead, many rural settlements are showing population growth, as people move there from urban areas. Rates of natural increase in richer countries are fairly stable, so the growth in the population of a particular settlement is generally due to in-migration.

14. Complete this summary table, using the phrases underneath.

Poorer Countries (LEDCs)	Richer Countries (MEDCs)

☐ high rates of natural increase   ☐ rapidly growing cities

☐ migration to rural areas   ☐ rural–urban migration

☐ low natural increase   ☐ growing rural settlements

Urban Growth in the UK

Today in the UK, 89 per cent of people live in towns and cities, but in 1780, only 25 per cent of the population lived in urban areas. Many of these people lived in London, which was the only big town by today's standards, with a population of 960 000 in 1801. At this time, many of today's cities, such as Birmingham, were just villages.

Much of the urban growth in the UK happened between 1730 and 1900. The cities grew for two main reasons:

1. *In-migration.* During the **Industrial Revolution**, thousands of people moved into the industrial towns to work in the new factories making goods such as cloth and metals (Resource 4.5). The main growth area was the central core of England – from South Lancashire and West Yorkshire through the Midlands to London. Also important were North East England and South Wales, plus Glasgow and Edinburgh in Scotland. Many people moved from nearby rural areas, but people also migrated from as far as Ireland to get jobs.

2. *Rapid natural increase.* Death rates were falling due to better diets, improved hygiene and disease control, but birth rates were still high. This resulted in a rapid growth rate, especially in the cities where many young people had moved. However, life was still not easy in the city – in Manchester in the 1880s, the average **life expectancy** was only 28.8 years.

The industrial towns grew quickly. For example, Liverpool's population increased from 34 407 in 1773 to 202 000 in 1831. The workers lived in **high density** terraced housing, owned by the factories and often poor quality (Resource 4.6). Some further migration carried on into the Twentieth Century – for example during the 1930s, many young girls from the poor mining valleys of South Wales moved to London to work as servants in the big houses. In 1911, only 21 per cent of people still lived in rural areas. There was much outward growth of cities during this century – with many semi-detached houses built along the main roads leading out of the cities, then large housing estates were built in the 1960s and 1980s, expanding urban areas even more. This outward growth is called **suburbanisation**.

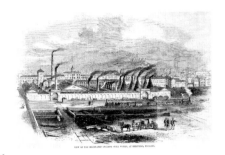

RESOURCE 4.5
Glasgow in the Industrial Revolution.

RESOURCE 4.6
Workers housing in Glasgow.

15. Why do you think life expectancy was so low in some cities?

16. Imagine you lived in the nineteenth century and have just moved into a large city to find work. Use the information and pictures on this page to write a letter home to your parents describing what life in the city is like. Is it what you expected?

Growth of rural areas in Britain

In Chapter 1, you studied the village of Leybourne in Kent. The village had undergone much change since a large estate was built in the 1980s (Resource 4.7), which joined it to other nearby settlements. The village grew because of the demand for new housing in country areas. It provided a pleasant environment within easy reach, by car or train, of London and other major employment centres. Many people moved there from urban areas, hoping to get a better quality of life.

RESOURCE 4.7
Idea for layout for Question 19.

The move away from urban areas to rural ones has been a constant trend in Britain since the 1960s. This move is called **counterurbanisation**. In-migration has particularly affected the rural areas of Southern England. For example, from 1981 to 1991, Dorset increased its population by 11.8 per cent, whilst Greater London declined by 4.9 per cent.

Improvements in transport such as motorways and high speed trains have made rural areas more accessible from urban areas. In some parts of rural Britain, this has created **commuter villages**. In these villages, the majority of residents work in urban areas, so are only present in the evenings and weekends. However, changes in technology such as electronic mail have meant that some people can work at home and only visit their firm's head office in the city occasionally.

17. Working with a partner, use an atlas and your general knowledge to suggest some reasons why Dorset's population should have grown, while Merseyside's declined.

18. Design a poster to show the advantages and disadvantages of the growth of rural villages. You could draw a village in the middle and put the writing round the edge (Resource 4.7). You may find it useful to brainstorm ideas as a class first. You could think about:

   ▪ Housing type and price
   ▪ Effects on services such as shops and schools
   ▪ Amount of open land available and quality of the environment
   ▪ Effects on the social life of the village
   ▪ Effects on the roads and public transport

How has rapid growth affected Bangkok?

Many cities in LEDCs have undergone massive growth caused by rural–urban migration and high rates of natural increase over the last 50 years. Bangkok, the capital of Thailand, grew from a population of under 1 million in 1940 to over 9 million in 1990. It covers an area of 7639 km². The city has been relatively successful in developing industry and jobs – 50 per cent of the nation's wealth is produced in Bangkok and the average income there is twice that in other areas of Thailand. Bangkok is also a major tourist centre with many attractions (Resource 4.8).

However, most of the city's growth was not planned, which means that Bangkok is facing various issues for the future:

- In 1985 there were 10 290 slum and squatter settlements in the city, housing around 1 million people. Some squatter settlements are very poor quality, temporary, and usually built illegally. The residents are often evicted and the area cleared so that new offices and housing can be built. Other areas of basic housing are more permanent, and some have services such as electricity. Many are built on stilts along the edges of the many *klongs* (canals) in the city. The largest squatter settlement called Klong Toey is located near the harbour and houses between 30–35 000 people.

- In 1987, only half the population of Bangkok had access to piped water. The demand for water has led to wells being built in the city. These wells are contributing to the soft soil subsiding – the city centre is sinking at a rate of 5–10 cm per year.

- Only 2 per cent of the city's population is connected to a mains sewage system. The rest of the people use cesspits and septic tanks or release the sewage straight into the waterways. This leads to health problems, particularly as the climate is hot and humid.

- The city cannot cope with the amount of rubbish it is producing. Each day 5400 tonnes of waste are produced and only 4200 tonnes are collected. The remaining rubbish blocks up the canals and causes pollution.

RESOURCE 4.8
Temple in Bangkok.

■ The growth of industry and population has been much faster than the growth and development of the road network. Bangkok has 80 per cent of the country's vehicles, but the roads cannot cope with them. It is estimated that in rush hours, the average speed of vehicles is less than 4 km/hour. The situation gets worse in the monsoon season, when heavy rain floods some roads. Many local people travel by boat along the canals (Resource 4.9)

■ A high proportion of the population has employment, although according to a 1985 survey, most adults are 'unskilled' workers. Many people work in informal services such as street trading. The income earned in this way may vary a lot from day to day, and there is no holiday or sick pay. There are often several income earners per household. This is necessary, because, as in most LEDCs, there is no Government support for people on low incomes.

The Government plans to construct 22 000 new units of housing and to upgrade 20 000, but this all requires funding. As the city grows outwards, the traffic problem will increase because more people need to commute to work in the centre. To reduce this pressure, the Government plans to encourage the building of housing for middle and high income groups nearer the centre.

RESOURCE 4.9
Boats on canal in Bangkok.

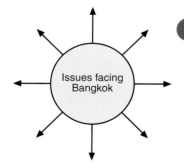

RESOURCE 4.10
Spider diagram.

20. Draw a large copy of the spider diagram and complete it to show the different issues facing Bangkok in the future. Try to include a fact to support each point:

21. Suggest a plan to the government to improve the quality of life for the poorer people in Bangkok. Focus on one or more of the issues you have identified. What reasons may prevent the Government carrying out your plan?

Why do some settlements decline?

Settlement decline is usually seen as a drop in the population of a settlement. This is called **depopulation**. Eventually the amount of space the settlement covers may decrease too, as abandoned houses decay.

The most likely reason for a settlement's population to decline is people moving away.

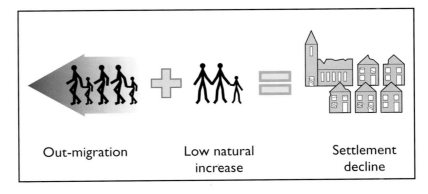

Out-migration   Low natural increase   Settlement decline

RESOURCE 4.11
Causes of settlement decline.

This is called **out-migration** (Resource 4.11). The population may drop further due to a low birth rate. Fewer babies are born because often the younger people have moved away to the city, leaving the settlement with mainly older people. This will also mean that the **death rate** would be higher than the birth rate, and the total population will fall. The population may also fall due to floods, droughts or wars, for example in the Korean War (1950–3), almost 1 million people in Korea were killed and much farmland destroyed. Population decline may cause problems for those left in the rural area as the number of people available to farm the land drops, which may lead to lower crop yields and even food shortages. There may not be enough customers for those working in service jobs.

In richer countries, many large cities have experienced depopulation since the 1960s. More remote rural areas have also declined.

22. a) Draw a line graph to show the population of London:

1961	8.0 million
1971	7.5 million
1981	6.7 million
1991	6.4 million

   b) Describe the pattern your graph shows.

   c) Predict what the population will be in the year 2000.

   d) Suggest some reasons why the population is changing in this way.

   e) How may this change affect the provision of services by the council which are paid for by local taxes?

23. Consider an urban area and a rural area you know. What evidence is there to indicate whether they are growing or declining? Why is the population changing in this way?

Why have some rural settlements declined in Britain?

RESOURCE 4.12
Abandoned croft in Skye.

We have already seen that in Britain, large urban areas are losing population as some people move out to find a better quality of life in the countryside. However, not all the UK's rural areas are growing – some more remote areas have experienced a drop in population over this century. For example in the Isle of Skye, the population fell from 14 619 in 1901 to 7 447 in 1981. In the previous century, the population reached over 20 000! This depopulation was originally due to changes in the farming system on the island, with amongst other factors, landowners evicting their tenants from their crofts. During the twentieth century, young people in particular drifted away from the island to areas offering an easier way of life (Resource 4.12). However, since 1981, as communications have improved and the tourist industry has developed, this trend has reversed and from 1981 to 1990, the population rose by 8 per cent.

A classic, though small scale, example of rural depopulation in Britain is the case of St Kilda. The four small islands in the St Kilda group (Resource 4.13) lie 177 km West of the Scottish mainland past the Outer Hebrides. The islands were very isolated – gales and storms meant it was very hard to land there from September to April. The main source of food was sea birds and their eggs, obtained by men climbing the dangerous cliffs. Sheep and some cows were also kept, but it was hard to grow crops. Feathers and tweed were exchanged for goods such as tea brought over from Skye once a year. The villagers lived in 25 small houses without services such as running water, electricity or mains sewage.

ATLANTIC OCEAN

St Kilda

Outer Hebrides

Inner Hebrides

SCOTLAND

ATLANTIC OCEAN

N

Stac an Armin

Boreray

Stac Lee

Soay
340m

ST KILDA

Glen Bay

Mullach Mhor
357m

Conachair
426m

Township dyke

Gleann Mhor

Amhuinn Mhor

Oiseval
289m

Mullach Bi
356m

Hirta

Church

Village Bay

Pier

Dun

0   km   1

RESOURCE 4.13
Location of St Kilda.

Despite their hard lifestyle, the community on St Kilda was very close and fair. None of the residents was in charge of the others, instead all the men met each morning to discuss the day's work and the food was shared out according to need. No crime was recorded for 400 years.

However, although the community on St Kilda had survived harsh conditions for at least 600 years, it was not able to survive in the twentieth century. The population had fallen from 180 in 1697 to 36 in 1930. This was mainly due to death rates being higher than birth rates and some islanders moving away to seek a better life elsewhere. Eventually it became hard for the community to survive – the soil was becoming too poor, there were fewer men to gather sea birds and the declining demand for produce such as feathers on the mainland meant it was hard to get supplies. After a particularly bad winter coping with illness and the threat of famine, the islanders decided to follow the advice of people from the mainland and were evacuated by the Government in 1930. The island is now owned by the National Trust for Scotland.

RESOURCE 4.14
Women on St. Kilda.

How does depopulation affect the rural area?

In St Kilda, depopulation eventually led to the island becoming deserted, but this is not always the case. In many LEDCs, high rural–urban migration has led to a reduction in the population of rural areas, but life there still continues. For example in Zambia, the rate of movement of people to the cities has been 1.2 per cent of the population since the 1960s. This has had various effects on the countryside:

- the men tend to migrate whilst the women stay to farm (Resource 4.15), leading to an imbalance between men and women in the countryside;
- there are fewer people left to farm, so the work is harder – it is difficult to get enough people to do essential tasks such as ploughing and harvesting;
- the decline in farming reduces profits, making it hard for farmers to buy ploughs or oxen which would make their farm better;
- the gap between rich and poor in rural areas is increasing;
- farmers have to try to increase their income by taking on further tasks such as basket-weaving, but this takes up valuable time;

RESOURCE 4.15
Women farmers in Africa.

Sometimes it is hard to know if anyone benefits from a family member going to the city to get work. In Cape Town, South Africa, migrants clearly have positive feelings towards the countryside, with many people going to visit relatives on a Sunday. Bongi's friends in the shanty town wish to earn money so that they can help the villages they came from. But how will they feel in 10 year's time when they have families of their own in Cape Town needing their help?

24. How do you feel that the old quality of life on St Kilda compares to your own?

25. Which push and pull factors caused the out-migration from St Kilda?

26. What are the similarities and differences between the rural depopulation in St Kilda and Zambia?

27. How could Governments help reduce rural depopulation?

Why do some urban areas decline?

Is it true that 'what goes up must come down'? The large urban areas which grew up in richer countries during the Industrial Revolution (see p. 39) certainly seem to be showing signs of slower population increase, and in many cases, a drop in population. The population of Liverpool fell by 13.5 per cent from 1981 to 1991. In America, Washington's population dropped by 8.3 per cent over 1980–92. However, this change does not affect all large urban areas in MEDCs to the same degree; New York's population actually grew by 3.4 per cent from 1980–92. Smaller urban areas are also continuing to grow, and growth of large urban areas in poorer countries continues to be rapid.

Some rural areas are growing because of counterurbanisation. The 'pull' to the countryside is easy to see. But is there also a 'push' from the big cities?

The heavy industry that made cities like Liverpool grow so much in the 1890s was not able to survive into the 1990s. Many of the big industries and large employers like ship building and steel making have either declined or closed down because they were unable to compete with other countries or lost their markets. This left inner city factories derelict, and the housing built for the workers was getting very run down. In Britain, many inner city areas were cleared in the 1950s and 60s, and the people were rehoused in new flats or edge of town estates. Many inner city areas still suffer from lack of employment, poor road access and social problems.

Although the total population of a city may decline, this change may not be evenly spread through the city – some areas will show more decline than others. For example, the population of Bristol has shown a steady decrease since the 1950s, but not all the areas within Bristol have declined (Resource 4.16).

RESOURCE 4.16
Population change in areas in Bristol.

Area	% population change 1951–71
1	+4
2	−24
3	−16
4	+588
5	−4
6	−40
7	−6
8	−11
9	−1
10	−39
11	−15
12	+118
13	−10
14	−17
15	15
16	−19
17	−7
18	+3
19	−34
20	−50
21	−68
22	−12
23	−5
24	−32
25	−7
26	+162
27	+28
28	−39

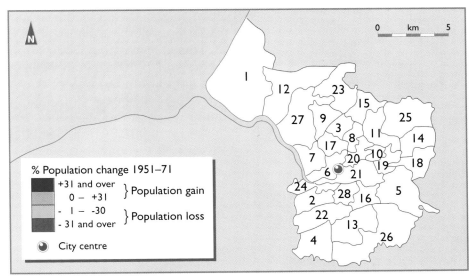

RESOURCE 4.17 Base map of Bristol.

28. On a copy of Resource 4.17, draw a map to show the information in Resource 4.16:

- Add the key to the bottom of your map.
- Colour each area on the base map in the correct colour according to the key. For example Area 1 would be coloured light blue.
- Give your map a title.

29. Which areas of Bristol have gained population?

30. Which areas have lost population?

31. Choose two areas and suggest some reasons why they have gained/lost people.

World Population Growth

We have seen in this chapter that populations in some areas of the world are growing, whilst other areas are declining. Overall, the world's population is very definitely on the increase. Until the nineteenth century, population growth was relatively slow, birth rates were just greater than death rates. However, with better food and medical care, birth rates rose significantly above death rates and overall growth was rapid. In richer developed countries, this growth has slowed down; the growth rate in the UK is 0.2 per cent per year. In many developing countries, the growth rate is still high; in Tanzania it is 3 per cent per year. Migration may also affect a country's population figure.

RESOURCE 4.18
Population pyramid for Brazil.

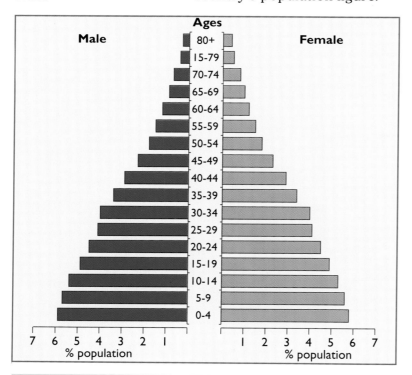

In Brazil, the rate of population increase is 2.1 per cent and the average number of children that each woman has is 3. This is fewer than it was 50 years ago, but, as can be seen in the population pyramid (Resource 4.18), there are many more younger people in the country, most of whom will later have their own families, so the population growth is likely to continue. In the UK, only 19 per cent of the population is aged 0–14, whilst 21 per cent is over 60. This keeps population growth at a slower level, but also has implications for healthcare and pensions as a larger proportion of the population has retired.

Population Factfile: Ethiopia
Total Population: 55 million
Birth Rate: 48 per 1000 per year
Death Rate: 18 per 1000 per year
Average number of children per woman: 7
Population aged 0–14: 45%
Life expectancy (male): 45 years

33. Why do you think that world population change is sometimes referred to as the 'population explosion'?

34. What would cause the world population growth to slow down? Should this happen?

35. Use evidence from the Factfile to predict what will happen to Ethiopia's population over the next century. Think of three reasons why this might not happen.

36. Write a short report to the Ethiopian government outlining the population trends in the country, suggesting ways of slowing down the growth and the possible consequences if this does not happen.

CHANGING SETTLEMENTS

5

Key Idea

The land in urban centres is not all office blocks. If you look around a city you will see that it is also a place where people live, where things are made, there are roads and shops and parks. Sometimes cities just grow like this, but this can cause problems. Usually there is a whole team of different planners who try to make living in the city a pleasant experience. What different factors do they look at?

Types and patterns of urban land use in MEDCs

There are many different types of land use within urban areas. These include:

- **residential areas** – housing – usually the quality of housing improves as you travel out from the centre of a town

- **industrial areas** – may be light industry (e.g. a small packaging firm), heavy industry (e.g. a steel works) or high-tech industry (e.g. scientific instruments)

- **commercial areas** – shops and offices – may be along main roads on the edge of town as well as in the town centre

- **open space** – from small recreation grounds to major parks and golf courses

- **transport links** – roads, railways and airports

RESOURCE 5.1
Land use in a typical MEDC city.

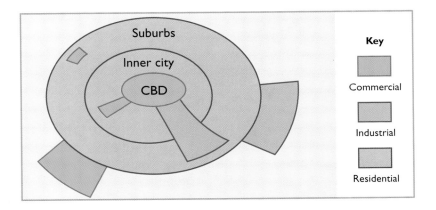

How can traffic problems in central urban areas be solved?

The number of vehicles on the roads in Britain has risen from 17 000 in 1903 to 25 million in 1992. However, many roads in CBDs and inner city areas were not built for this amount of traffic, leading to problems of congestion, lack of parking space, noise, pollution and conflict between cars and pedestrians.

Five solutions to traffic difficulties are shown below:

- **Traffic calming** – aims to slow down the traffic passing through residential areas to reduce noise and the risk of accidents. Can include speed bumps, further speed restrictions and road narrowing. May also aim to reduce through traffic because the traffic calming measures are time consuming to pass through.

- **Pedestrianisation** – all or most vehicles are banned from travelling down certain roads. The ban may be permanent or for a certain time each day. This is most likely in city centre shopping areas to improve the environment for shoppers.

- **Bypasses** – a **ring road** is built round the edge of the city. This means that travellers who would previously have had to go through the town centre can now go round the edge. This reduces journey times and congestion in the town centre. However, bypasses are expensive to build and sometimes controversial because they go through areas which people consider should be left as open space.

- **Park and Ride Schemes** – large car parks are built near the edge of the town for people to leave their cars free of charge. A free or low cost bus service then runs people into the town centre. City centre parking prices may sometimes be increased to encourage people to use the park and ride schemes.

- **Improvements in public transport** – buses or trams are considered more efficient ways of moving people around, but they are less flexible to use for individuals than cars. Cycle lanes may be appropriate in some areas of cities.

1. Draw a sketch map of your area and label on any traffic improvements. Evaluate their success.

2. Why is public transport better for the environment than private cars? What are the disadvantages of using public transport?

Changes in the rural–urban fringe in MEDCs

The **rural–urban fringe** is the area on the edges of towns and cities where the urban area ends and the rural area begins. Sometimes the border line is obvious, but sometimes it's not so easy to pick out, particularly if the town has grown outwards to touch villages, as we saw with Leybourne in Chapter 1. All urban areas in richer countries have experienced outward growth of fairly good quality, low density housing over the twentieth century. This suburbanisation has continued in many cities even though the overall population levels have declined. The edges of towns have experienced other types of development as well as housing estates, as industrial estates, science parks and shopping centres have also been built. Road links such as bypasses also need the open land at the edge of the urban area.

RESOURCE 5.7
The M25 around London was built through Green Belt land.

In the 1940s, the Government in Britain became concerned that urban areas would sprawl too far out into the countryside, so they planned a series of **Green Belts** around major cities. A Green Belt is an area of mainly open land surrounding the city where it is difficult to get permission for any new buildings. London had the first Green Belt and now at least 31 cities in the UK have one. However, it is not impossible to build in a Green Belt as buildings associated with rural land uses such as farming and outdoor sports facilities are often allowed.

Generally Green Belts have achieved their aim of limiting the outward growth of major urban areas. However, building restrictions on the edges of cities can often cause pressure for development within the city itself as any spare land is filled up with housing.

3. Why do you think planners felt that a Green Belt was necessary around London?

4. Does your local urban area have a Green Belt? Do you think it needs one?

How is central Berlin changing?

The central areas of most cities have changed a lot over the last 40–50 years. CBDs have had to accommodate new ideas in shopping, new demands on office space and new expectations of environmental quality and transport links. Inner city areas have experienced the economic, social and environmental effects of the decline of industry. New shopping centres and office blocks have been built in CBDs and new high rise flats have followed slum clearance in many inner city areas. In some cities, parts of the inner city have become popular places to live and the terraced houses have been improved by new owners (gentrification).

In the late 1990s, Berlin seems to be experiencing all of these changes at the same time. In fact when counted in 1996 there were over 320 major building sites, mainly on the old East Berlin side, with 1200 cranes (Resource 5.5). This redevelopment has been encouraged by the German Government's decision to move their parliament back to Berlin from Bonn in 2000. The parliamentary building has to be rebuilt and Government-related functions such as foreign embassies all need buildings and transport facilities. Many of the old East Berlin buildings were in a very poor state of repair and were not suitable to be part of a new capital for the twenty-first century.

One major project is the Potsdamer Platz. This big square was the centre of life in Berlin before the war, but after the war it became a wasteland on the border between East and West Berlin. Now companies such as Daimler, Mercedes Benz and Sony are spending over £1.5 billion developing a shopping and office complex, which should be finished by 1998 (Resource 5.5).

The building sites in Berlin are proving very popular with tourists! It was not unusual for these sites to have up to 60 000 visitors each weekend, many on organised tours.

RESOURCE 5.5a
Potsdamer Platz, Berlin.

The new companies seem pleased at the interest and have joined with the local government to provide a visitor centre for tourists. In the 'Info-Box', tourists can see information about what the finished area will look like, as well as getting a good view of the current building work, including the 1800 tonne Emperor's Hall being moved 75 metres on a cushion of air to become the centre of the new Sony building! Change isn't only happening in the city centre; at Karow in North East Berlin, 15 000 homes are being built.

The building sites have also become a pull factor for immigrant workers. In 1996, 200 000 construction workers were estimated to have moved into the city from abroad, many illegally. Ten to sixty thousand of these workers come from Britain, but there were also Dutch, Poles, Russians, Bosnians, Turks, Irish, Italian and Portuguese workers, as well as Germans. Most immigrants worked longer hours for lower wages than the Germans, but still made more money than they would have done in their home countries. However, the German government is concerned that the immigrants provide a cheaper workforce, undermining the German standard of wages, and possibly raising unemployment for Germans.

5. Imagine you are visiting Berlin and are standing on the viewing platform of the 'Info-Box'. Write a postcard to a friend back home describing what you can see.

6. Why do you think tourists are so interested in the building sites?

7. How might the changes in Berlin affect the city in the next 10 years? Think about environmental quality, jobs, population and social mix.

RESOURCE 5.5b
Potsdamer Platz, Berlin.

Would Cambridge benefit from further growth in the computer industry?

Cambridge has a strong history of growth in the field of High-Tech industry (modern, scientific research and manufacturing). This growth started when Trinity College established the Cambridge Science park (Resource 5.8) on the northern edge of the city in 1972. Many firms specialising in computer hardware, software and Information Technology are now based in Cambridge. The area is popular with these firms for various reasons:

- links with the university are possible
- good environmental quality
- good housing and schools to attract a high quality workforce
- good links with London and airports.

However, various issues are associated with this growth. Congestion is an on-going problem – access to the science park and town centre can be slow in rush hours.

Due to the pressures for growth of high-tech industry, most of the possible development sites within the city have been taken. The main area for future growth will have to be the rural–urban fringe in Cambridge's green belt or between the northern edge of Cambridge and the A14.

RESOURCE 5.8
Cambridge Science Park.

In the summer of 1997, Microsoft, a major computer firm, announced that it would be working with Cambridge University to set up a research base in the city. The company plans to invest £50 million in the research centre as well as investing £10 million in other new technology projects, with an emphasis on using local companies. The research centre intends to employ 40 people on a permanent site proposed to be in the West Cambridge area.

8. What do you think the reactions of the people of Cambridge would be to this proposal. What would they be pleased about? What might they worry about? What questions would they have?

WHAT EFFECTS MIGHT GROWTH HAVE?

The general reaction to the announcement was enthusiastic, though there were some concerns about further growth. It is important not to exaggerate the impact that the research centre itself could have. Forty new jobs will bring some new families into the area needing housing and transport, and the centre will need land. The newspaper article (Resource 5.9) is concerned about what will happen if other technology and computing firms are encouraged to come to Cambridge by its connection with Microsoft attracting another 1000 jobs.

It is not unusual for one place which is successful for a particular industry to attract other firms. In Seattle, in north west USA, where Microsoft started in 1974, the company now employs 12 000 people. The average house price in central Seattle rose from around £63 000 in 1989 to around £150 000 partly as a result of increased demand from a growing population attracted by the new jobs in the computer industry.

Microsoft 'could cause new strains'

A NEW surge of companies and workers into Cambridge that could follow Microsoft's planned move to the city would threaten the already strained infrastructure, warns a leading business figure.

Most companies have welcomed Microsoft's plans, announced at the end of last week, to set up a research centre tapping into university expertise.

And the majority thought the competition provided by Microsoft would stimulate business in the region rather than damage it.

But the possibility of another 1000 employees travelling to and working in Cambridge is worrying some people.

Walter Herriot, director of St John's Innovation Centre in Cambridge, said: "Microsoft coming here has got to be a good thing if it benefits the university.

"But it's very important to consider the effect on house prices, transport, schools and the rest.

"If the new site is going to be in the west of Cambridge you need to ask how everybody is going to get

off the motorway at junction 13.

"They are already backing up on to the motorway and a few hundred extra cars are going to make it considerably worse."

Mr Herriot said although Microsoft would provide competition for jobs and may be acquisitive, Cambridge companies were strong enough to survive.

"It may create some problems but if Microsoft go elsewhere we would not get the benefits."

Cambridge Evening News,
3 June 1997

RESOURCE 5.9
Article from Cambridge
Evening News

9. Using Resource 5.9, make a table of the possible advantages and disadvantages for Cambridge of further growth in the computer industry.

10. Why should growth in jobs cause house prices to rise?

11. Think of one group of people who would benefit from the growth of new industry and one group who might lose out.

IS THERE ENOUGH SPACE FOR NEW GROWTH IN CAMBRIDGE?

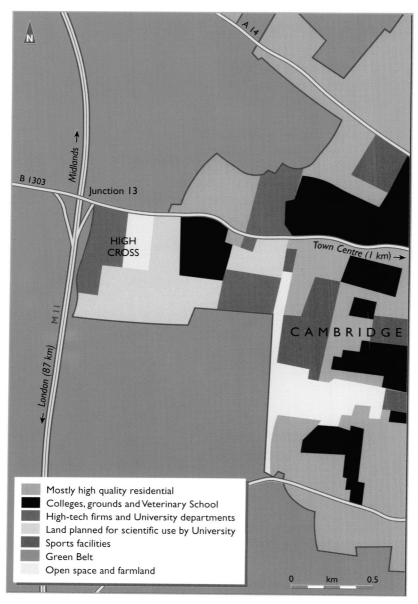

Legend:
- Mostly high quality residential
- Colleges, grounds and Veterinary School
- High-tech firms and University departments
- Land planned for scientific use by University
- Sports facilities
- Green Belt
- Open space and farmland

RESOURCE 5.10
Land use in West Cambridge.

Microsoft intends to find a site in West Cambridge for its new research centre. Space is limited on this side of Cambridge as much of the land inside the green belt is already taken up by housing and the University (Resource 5.10). The area is close to the M11 for access to London, though Junction 13 only allows traffic to enter the M11 in a southbound direction and leave in a northbound direction, so access to the Midlands is slightly less direct. There are a number of modern firms already situated at High Cross in West Cambridge, including British Antarctic Survey and Schlumberger (Resource 5.11). Future development in West Cambridge near the Microsoft base might not be possible without expanding into the green belt.

RESOURCE 5.11
Schlumberger Building, High Cross, Cambridge.

12. Describe the pattern of land use shown on the map.

13. Decide where on the map you would recommend the Microsoft Research centre to locate. What would the advantages and disadvantages of the site be for Microsoft?

14. If you were a city councillor, would you support further development in green belt land? Explain your decision.

THE DECISION

Even if a company's proposed site isn't in a Green Belt, it won't automatically get permission to build from the local council. First of all it has to apply to the local planning department. The planners then spend time considering the application in relation to Structure plans for the area. During this process, they consult with people who might be affected by the development, by writing to people and putting up notices at the proposed site. If the proposal is likely to cause strong feelings amongst some local groups (Resource 5.12), a public meeting may be arranged so the proposals can be explained in more detail and everyone's views can be heard. At the end of the period of consultation, the planners recommend to the planning committee of the local council whether the development should go ahead. Planning permission is then either given or refused.

RESOURCE 5.12
People protesting against the new runway at Manchester airport.

If the Council refuses planning permission, the developers can appeal to the Secretary of State to have the decision reconsidered. The Government may then set up a **public enquiry**, where all interested groups can give their views. This usually only happens with major developments such as power stations and bypasses as it is a lengthy and expensive process. Eventually the Secretary of State will decide whether the project should be allowed to go ahead and this decision is final. In Microsoft's case, a suitable, moderately sized site which is not on Green Belt land is likely to be approved.

15. Draw a flow diagram to show the process of applying for planning permission. You will need to draw a box for each step, then join up the boxes with arrows.

e.g.

16. Do you think further growth of the computing industry in Cambridge should be encouraged? Why/why not?

Types and patterns of urban land use in LEDCs

RESOURCE 5.13
Typical city structure in South America.

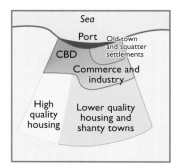

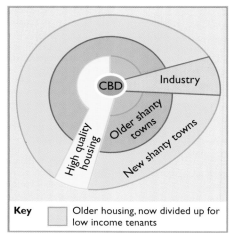

Key ▢ Older housing, now divided up for low income tenants

The general types of land use in cities in LEDCs are the same as those we have identified in MEDCs – including residential areas, commercial areas and industry. However, typical land use patterns in the two types of cities are quite different.

Resources 5.13 and 5.14 show typical city structures in South America and South East Asia.

RESOURCE 5.14
Typical city structure in South East Asia.

RESOURCE 5.15
Panjim Goa, India

Remember that these types of maps are quite general – all cities have their own characteristics and their land use patterns will not be exactly the same as these. The sections on Manila (p. 25) and Lima (p. 23) have more detailed city maps.

The South American map (Resource 5.13) is based on a city growing outwards from the CBD in a series of concentric rings. The older, more established housing is nearer the centre and the more recent shanty towns are around the edges. As rural–urban migration and high natural increase continue, the city spreads outwards. Industry forms a wedge pattern from the centre because it is along a good transport link such as a main road. Some higher income groups live near the CBD because access to jobs and cultural facilities is good. The areas of better quality housing are also growing outwards – often towards the coast if the city is near the sea. The South East Asian map (Resource 5.14) has some similarities to Resource 5.13, but because most large cities in South East Asia are ports, growth is limited on the seaward side. In both cities, shanty towns are mixed in with other land uses across the city, but the largest areas of low income housing are towards the edges of the city where there is more land available.

RESOURCE 5.16
Bhopal, India

17. Describe the types of land use shown in Resources 5.15 and 5.16. Suggest a location for each one on the city maps shown in Resources 5.13 or 5.14

18. Give two ways in which urban land use patterns in MEDCs and LEDCs are similar and two ways they are different.

Can Quality of Life in cities in LEDCs be improved?

As we saw in the case of Lima (p. 23), the major issue for cities in LEDCs is not that everyone is poor – rather that there is a massive gap between the rich minority and the poor majority. In Bangkok (p. 41) and Manila (p. 25) the difficulties of inadequate housing and services for the people living in squatter settlements resulted from rapid unplanned growth. As rural–to–urban migration continues, it is sometimes hard to see hope for improvements in the future. In many cities, the local authorities and various charities are working to improve the situation for the poorer people. Sometimes the local authority upgrades shanty towns by providing piped water or electricity. In other areas there are site and services schemes where people can rent a small plot of land which has links to electricity and water supplies. They then build their own house on this plot. However, the problems of low incomes and poor transport systems are very hard to solve.

The city of Curitiba in southern Brazil grew from a population of 500 000 in 1971 to 1.6 million in 1992. The city has experienced the problems of crime and poverty associated with high rural–to–urban migration – one third of residents earned less than $200 per month in 1996. Jaime Lerner, the mayor of the city since 1971 and now the state governor believes 'The poorer you are, the better services you should have'. He has worked with the city planners to develop some inventive ways of improving services, such as transport, at a relatively low cost.

RESOURCE 5.17
The transport system in Curitiba.

The first main scheme was to improve the transport system which was slow and inefficient. Large, modern buses are the focus of the system (Resource 5.17). The service is fast because the buses travel in special lanes on the roads and people buy tickets at the bus stops before they travel. Bus stops are located every 400 m along the routes and there is access for disabled people. The scheme has been very successful – 80 per cent of people travel to work by bus.

RESOURCE 5.18
Exchanging recycled waste for food in Curitiba.

Recycling waste materials is very important within the city. Low income families can exchange recyclable waste for food once a fortnight (Resource 5.18). Four kg of waste can be swapped for 1 kg of food such as fruit and vegetables, which are bought at a fair price from local farmers. This scheme gives people a better diet and reduces the risk of disease and flooding from rubbish dumped in waterways. Nearly 70 per cent of the city's waste is now recycled.

The city is also trying to improve services and the environment in the shanty towns. Schools are being built on the edges of the town to provide education and job training for local residents. Tree planting is promoted and there are large quantities of public open space. The larger parks have picnic sites, swimming and boating areas and nature trails.

These schemes have not provided instant solutions to all the city's problems, but they do provide signs of hope and a way of involving the local community in the future of the city.

19. What are the main problems that cities in poorer countries face? How many of these are being addressed in Curitiba by the schemes outlined above?

20. Why do you think the city chose to promote buses as the major form of transport in Curitiba?

21. Do you think any of the schemes would work well in cities in richer countries? Explain why/why not.